The Angelic Scripts

Kelsey McManis

The Angelic Scripts

By
Kelsey McManis

Edited by
Arielle Hadfield

Copyright@ 2024

Preface

   How many times have we been told to let the person of our hearts know that we love them? Well, now is the time to act on all we've learned, like the knights of old. We can prove our love for each other, be the men, women, sons, daughters, husbands, and wives we know that we should and can be, all of the good things we want to be, by writing little notes every day, sending texts over the phone or messages of any kind to our friends and family. Have we ever thought of writing letters to express ourselves? This collection of letters, or maybe even journal entries, is just that. Things felt, but never said, were inspired by a great and noble woman who once told a man that he never cries. Could this be just because he's a man?

Perhaps he just doesn't know how to express himself or his feelings about her or any feelings. The letters may not express your feelings, thoughts, or emotions, but they will be written from man to woman and back again. I feel as though they are trying to express both sides of the heart and mind. We as humans sometimes misunderstand one's lack of emotions as not loving or caring for the other person. I'm not sure how these letters even found their way to my family, but they did. Perhaps there's a heavenly mail person or some kind of delivery system in place. God is grand in his plan to help us along our way here on this Earth.

Please feel free to be sad, be glad, feel loved, or even cry at times. After all, we are here to learn from our mistakes and become better and help others for good. If while reading this you start thinking, "Oh poor me. I'm divorced, single, widowed, or the worst, no one loves me and I'm not capable of being loved," then search your heart, mind, and soul. Coming from a Christian background, I'd advise you to go to your knees and ask the good Lord our Heavenly Father to help you find the answers you are searching for. Everyone deserv**es** to be happy and find joy in being loved, and in return, loving someone. We all have seen those couples of all races who are old and have been married for as long as we can imagine. We know and hopefully at some point realize that we all make mistakes, but we also desire to have our happiness. Every happy and great relationship takes work from everyone.

Kelsey McManis June 2023

Letter One

My Dearest and Loving Wife,

   Things I've felt but never said to you: I sit here after all of these years of being married to you, my feelings and thoughts are so many. Being the man I am, I've not told you all of my feelings for you. They are so many, as my love for you has grown a million-fold over the years. This morning I woke up before you even stirred. I just laid there watching over you as you slept, looking so peaceful. There are so many things I wish I could have done better for you. You have told me more than once or twice over the years that I've never cried. Well, I'm not pouring my feelings out to you through this short letter. My love, please let me start with how much my heart breaks every time we have a difference of our minds. You know how much I love peace and harmony. I feel as though I'm going to die from the harsh words we both say to one another. I live to see every time you brighten up my life with your beautiful smile. Your eyes sparkle as fireworks of joy are going off in your heart. The fight we had last night about how to cook roast beef was so stupid. While I still don't agree with you, I realize that neither of us was right or wrong. Knowing this should help both of us remember that nobody is always right. We can try things your way first, and if we both decide we don't like it that way, we can try them my way and decide which one we like better. My love for you will never change, only how I express it. I hope this letter finds you in better feelings and much happiness.

  Love always, Husband

Letter Two
To My Handsome Husband,

Well, that wasn't half bad for your first letter, I will always love you. You've always been a man of few words and a lot of actions showing me how much you love me—from doing the laundry, dishes, and making dinner when I'm too tired. I will give you this bit of advice though. Next time if you don't know how to cook something, please Google it. You can find anything on the internet. I will forgive you this time and every time, as I love seeing you trying to make it up to me. You're so cute when you want to show me your love. I love how much you are always trying to find new ways of pouring out your heart to me. I've enjoyed every day of waking up before you and watching over you also. The day we met, I told myself that this man would need a lot of taming and teaching. I also hate our fighting and not being of the same mind as one another. I realized this as I lay there in our bed and you were down on the couch. Oh, how I'm so excited to pour my heart to you in this new way for us. Through letters to each other, it will help us to find different words to express ourselves one with another. I love your smile when you're happy and full of joy. The way you take my hand, twirling me around with no music, dancing through the house, I feel like a teenager all over again. All you do is talk and tell me words and sometimes show me the actions of your love.

I want more from our relationship, if you do indeed plan on staying married to me. Perhaps a date night once a week or even come to bed at the same time. I love you and want to spend more time with the man I fell in love with when we were teenagers.

Maybe, love your wife more

Journal One
Journal entry of a husband

Today we started the fall of 1959, and I woke up turning to my nightstand seeing a folded up letter. I opened it up. The letter was from my lovely wife. Wow, she wrote a longer letter than I did. How she ended the letter saying I need to show her that I love *maybe love your wife more*, now that stuck out to me like a sore thumb. She is right though. her more often. She also gave me a lot of great ideas to go about showing her my love for her.

The years have flown and really gotten away from me. I

know I can't be the only one who feels this way. I feel as if my life here on this earth is about to come to a sudden end, and I should start preparing myself to see my God.

After several years of not finishing this entry, I'll choose to continue and finish it. After talking to my father and mother about this and having been away on mission helping other couples to be happy, show love, be friendly toward one another, and saying no to all that is bad, I love my eternal wife even more than ever. You see, we are angels now, and that one night and the next morning were our last on the Earth as mortals.

As a side note, we aren't the first ones to try and help couples and families be happy and stay together. I guess our God, or as I love to call him, our Father, chose us because we knew everything the Devil would and could use to destroy families. So I will include all our letters and journal entries in this instruction book to new angels who get assigned to help families for good.

There will be all sorts of different case studies in this, such as couples both brought up in the belief of God, a husband or wife who finds themselves addicted to all sorts of things on the internet, and other things. Also racism is a very bad thing and will tear the hearts of the human race apart from each other. Peace, love, and kindness to our brothers and sisters here on this Earth will help us get along one with another.

Journal Two

Journal entry by an angel aka a wife.

While this wasn't a surprise to me that I was chosen to help other couples, teenagers, and the elderly, my husband of forty odd years was chosen to be my teammate yet again. Now God did not let this slip by him, but gave us the council that being a couple that doesn't think the same as each other is a gift. We could and would use all of what we learned and gained in the way of knowledge and wisdom to help others. I will say that sometimes husbands can be a pain in the royal backside. We love them most of the time. Even that thought makes me giggle inside because truth told, we always love them. Men do not always think like women, and that can lead them to anger, wrong decision making, and getting addicted to things. I'm scared and excited for my first assignment as an angel or guiding light. We all need counsel, and a guiding light is very helpful at times when we get lost. I love everyone as my sisters and brothers on this ride called life. Our souls, or as some call them, our spirits, are all all created equal. Our mortal bodies, or the shell that houses our soul, are different colors and from different parts of the Earth. On Earth we speak different languages, but in Heaven we all speak the same language.

Letter Five
To the angels helping couples,

    I love each one of you with all of my heart, and I know that you will be able to perform your assigned duties, to help others stay together and find the good in each other. Just some teaching that each couple should spend at least one night a week for about one or two hours as a family and one night with their spouse on a date of their choice. Love and sparks need to be present within the marriage so that their love for each other can grow stronger. Their job as a couple is to raise good and great children who obey the law of their lands and my laws. These laws are only for the good of all men and women. Beware of adversity among the couples, family, and other people of all races. There will be races fighting against each other, couples losing faith in each other, people choosing addictions over what is right and family. Remember to help others pray and always be believing, for I will always be there to help and guide everyone back to me. In closing, I would like to advise you that I know both of you will do great and you should never be afraid to write to me for advice or help.

I offer my help because I know your job will be hard and difficult at times.
   Love, Father

Letter Six

Dear Father,

I can't believe this husband, he is terrible. All he does is watch sports, TV shows, and play on his phone. He comments how the white guy is better than the black guy and doesn't understand that we are all created equal, each with different talents and skills. He spends no time whatsoever with his wife or children, like a great husband and dad should. How do I get him to realize what he is missing out on? I can see that his wife loves him with all of her heart and desires to stay with him, but only if changes. I need help with this one Father! Please help me!

From,
Angel Husband

Letter Seven

My Son and Angel Husband,

I've given this much thought and have come up with a way of helping you, but without doing it for you. You need to do this on your own with my teachings about families. Families are an important part in my grand plan of happiness, along with the Atonement of my son Jesus Christ. First, you must go into the wife's thoughts as she prays, giving her hope that he will start praying with her and change. Then while the husband is sleeping, go into his dreams and show him possible future he has without his family if he keeps these choices up. He will end up in jail, alone, or worse, dead, if he keeps thinking that white lives matter more than anyone else. All lives matter and can work together. Let him know that he is loved very much by his whole family and myself. Lastly, show him the future he will have with his family if he chooses them first above anything. He will amount to nothing without his family and cannot be who is meant to be.

Love, Father

Letter Eight

My Darling Husband,

  I realize you care about everyone and want everyone to be happy. Sometimes you just need to teach them by your thoughts and example. You are a great spirit and do great. God has given you a lot of great wisdom and ideas for helping others. Please listen to him and remember that you cannot force anyone to do what is right. You must always give them the opportunity to choose what is right and good on their own. Know that I love you and also I know that you can do this. Just believe at all times and know that God is real and Christ has died for us. Because of this, we can be forgiven of our sins if we really repent with all of our heart and mind. He was also resurrected so that we could be with our families forever. Please let the wife and husband know these pieces of joy. Because God lives outside of our known understanding of time, he let me help a young man in the year 1959 who also played high school football, like you did. This story may or may not help you. This young man and a few of his teammates were on a trip to play a game in another town in the state of Missouri. They had one black player on their team and decided to walk into a diner to have fries and shakes. The manager of that diner told them that they don't serve the young mans kind. The teammates just looked at each other and quietly made the decision together to just walk out. The young black boy asked them why they did that for him and their answer will surprise you. They answered that they are a team and stand together as a team. So my husband, there are already people in this world who love others and treat them equally with friendship and love.

   Love, Your Angel Wife

Letter Nine

Dear Father,

   This is angel wife, and I have a major concern about the family I'm working with. The wife of my family is feeling like she is not loved by anyone in the family. The husband is doing everything he can to show her that he loves and cares about her. He helps her with the meals, the cleaning, and also helps their children with their school work. The kids love her and are saddened by her state of mind. I've been in her dreams and shown her that her family loves and cares for her and wants to be with her always and forever. I've done my best to be by her side holding her hand, letting her know that someone is there with her. However, she still feels like she is drowning in a sea of sorrow. What should I do to help her realize that life is worth living? How can I further help her?

  From, Angel Wife

Letter Ten

Angel Wife,

I've read your letter and understand your concern about the wife. I would advise you to go to her other family members, such as her brothers and sisters, along with her friends. They may be able to help her feelings and thoughts of despair. You're doing a great job, please keep it up. This should help you and perhaps you can also urge her to read the Bible, helping her to remember that she is not alone in the world.

Love, Father

Letter Eleven

Dear People Living on Earth,

  My love goes out to you in whatever situation that you're going through right now. Remember that I'm always here waiting and wanting to listen to you and help you and your families. Please remember that you should and need to love and be kind to everyone no matter what. I know that at times it can be very hard to do, but if you remember that they are your brothers and sisters and are equal to you, this will help you. Only you can choose the decisions for yourself, so realize that you will either get

rewarded or you will receive consequences. There is always a choice between right and wrong, good or evil, and best or better. Please choose wisely.
       Love, Father

Letter Twelve

Our Dearest Earthly Children,

    Our Heavenly Father has allowed me write you this letter, truly I know and realize that it's been years since we have left our mere mortal Earthly lives. Your father and I are very sorry for the way we may have left you and know that there is still so much more we want and feel that we need to teach you to survive on Earth and in our Fathers kingdom. We love all of you and know that only one of you will truly follow your heart and spirit to help guide your family in all that is good and righteous. You have come from a great lineage and are of royal blood. I don't mean the blood of the Earth, but of the Heavens.....even God himself. You need to know that there is more to life than just work, fun, parties, and TV. Our Father in Heaven has a great plan of Happiness for all of us, and He really desires that you find it or continue upon the path. He may teach you in many different ways such as, but not limited to, dreams, others who you may come into contact with, scripture, nature, and even music. Please, I beg of you to go to him in prayer in the name of our Savior Jesus

Christ and thank him for all that is good and great in your lives. Then ask him what He has in store for you so that you can help others in their quest to find God and follow him. Love one another.

Love,

Your Angel Mother

Letter Thirteen

Our Earthbound Children,

    You should know that you are stronger together, but that one of you will be leader among all of you. Your mother and I plead with our Father quite often to give you great gifts and talents that can help you upon your journey on the Earth. You should always help each other and keep in some sort of contact with each other so that you can better help one another. We love you all of the time and can't wait to see you again when that time comes.

  Love, Your Angel Dad

Notes From The Author

Even though we have lost someone dear and close to our hearts and each of our lives. We can still learn
and feel inspired from them, by reading their journals, letters to others, and their own history. So I beg of you, no I really encourage you to know your family, even the ones that have past on to the next life and even those that you never knew. There are many ways to go about this, talking to other family members that may have a history to hand down to you. Also you can do your very own genealogy.

We can learn from everything, even the dead, and books. Books tell a great and marvelous story in themselves. What you put in your mind and heart is all up to you, so be very mindful of what
you read and learn.

About The Author

Kelsey McManis is a man of vision and imagination, values God, family and learning about history from great books. In August of 1976 he was born in Kansas City Missouri to two great parents and was raised in Overland Park Kansas. While attending Shawnee Mission South High School he continued his yearning for learning and reading. He has been influenced by the great storytellers of olden and modern time through out his life. Moving to Utah he met his beautiful and wonderful wife and together they have six children and eight grandchildren. Kelsey plans for the future and so attended BYU Idaho online and received a certificate in Social Media Management. kmcmanis@yahoo.com

Also By Kelsey McManis
Coming Soon

Infinities Bloodline vol 1

August 2024
Infinities Bloodline vol 2
Infinities Bloodline Travel Guide